Mysterious Rain Forests

KINGFISHER

NEW YORK

KINGFISHER
LONDON & NEW YORK

Copyright © Macmillan Publishers International Ltd 2016
Published in the United States by Kingfisher,
175 Fifth Ave., New York, NY 10010
Kingfisher is an imprint of Macmillan Children's Books, London
All rights reserved.

Distributed in the U.S. and Canada by Macmillan,
175 Fifth Ave., New York, NY 10010

Library of Congress Cataloging-in-Publication data
has been applied for.

Interior design by Tall Tree Ltd
Cover design by Peter Clayman

Adapted from an original text by Claire Llewellyn
Literacy consultants: Kerenza Ghosh, Stephanie Laird

Illustrations by Barry Coucher and Gary Hanna/www.the-art-agency.co.uk, Peter Bull Art Studio

ISBN 978-0-7534-7253-8 (HB)
ISBN 978-0-7534-7248-4 (PB)

Kingfisher books are available for special promotions
and premiums. For details contact: Special Markets
Department, Macmillan, 175 Fifth Ave.,
New York, NY 10010.

For more information, please visit
www.kingfisherbooks.com

Printed in China

9 8 7 6 5 4 3 2 1
1TR/1115/WKT/UG/128MA

Contents

Forest layers

Inside a rain forest, huge trees tower up into a mass of leaves high above. The air is hot and very humid because there is heavy rain every day. The conditions are perfect for plants to grow—and these plants are home to a huge variety of animals.

The quetzal was worshiped by the ancient Aztec people, who lived in Mexico.

Canopy

A rain forest has several layers. At the top is the **canopy** of leaves. There is more sunlight up here, and the trees grow fruits and seeds throughout the year. Most animals live in the canopy because there is plenty of food.

The Queen Alexandra's birdwing is the largest butterfly in the world, with wings up to 11 inches (28 centimeters) across.

Understory

Stretching between the canopy and the ground is the **understory**. Plants grow larger leaves to catch whatever light they can reach. With fewer branches, there is space for insects and birds to fly. **Reptiles** such as snakes move along the tree trunks.

The jaguar hunts for prey in rivers as well as on the forest floor.

The giant leaf-tailed gecko has a flat tail shaped like a leaf. It stands up and hisses loudly when threatened.

Forest floor

There is very little light here, and few plants can grow. Leaves and other litter fall from the trees above and cover the ground, where they rot down quickly in the humid conditions. Huge numbers of insects live among the **leaf litter**, including ants and termites. A few large **mammals**, such as anteaters and jaguars, hunt for food on the forest floor.

The mandrill is one of the most colorful of all mammals, with bright blue and red swellings on the face and rump.

The rafflesia plant has the world's largest flowers, up to 35 inches (90 centimeters) across. The plant produces a smell of rotting meat in order to attract flies that will **pollinate** it.

TOP FIVE BITESIZE FACTS

- More **species** of wildlife live in rain forests than in any other place on Earth.

- This **habitat** is under threat as areas are cleared for farms, mines, and roads.

- Many canopy animals never go down to the forest floor.

- Only about 5 percent of sunlight reaches the understory.

- Tall trees poking above the canopy are called **emergents**.

humid
Moist or damp (in the air).

The world's rain forests

Most rain forests lie between the **tropics** of Capricorn and Cancer. Here the sun is hottest and the rainfall is highest. These are known as the tropical rain forests, but there are also temperate rain forests in cooler parts of the world.

NORTH AMERICA

The American black bear is one of the largest mammals living in the temperate rain forests of Canada and Alaska.

KEY

temperate rain forest

tropical rain forest

AFRICA

Atlantic Ocean

Pacific Ocean

Amazon rain forest

Tropic of Capricorn

SOUTH AMERICA

Rain forest belts

There are three major belts of tropical rain forests across the world. The largest covers the basins of the Amazon and Orinoco rivers in South America. The others are along the Congo River in Africa and from Myanmar to New Guinea in Southeast Asia.

temperate
Parts of the world that lie between the tropics and the polar regions.

The estuarine crocodile lives in saltwater areas on the coasts of Southeast Asia and Australia. It is the world's largest crocodile.

ASIA

The Iban people of Sarawak, Malaysia, build wooden longhouses on stilts that keep them high above river floods.

EUROPE

Tropic of Cancer

Pacific Ocean

Southeast Asia

AUSTRALIA

Indian Ocean

Equator

The massive Eastern lowland gorilla can be found only in the tropical forests of the Congo in Central Africa.

TOP FIVE BITESIZE FACTS

🍃 Temperate forests are kept damp not just by rain, but also by ocean or mountain fogs.

🍃 The biggest temperate rain forest is on the Pacific coast of North America.

🍃 Rain forests cover only 2 percent of Earth's total surface area, but are home to half of the planet's plants and animals.

🍃 The UK and Ireland would fit into the Amazon rain forest 17 times.

🍃 Plants in the Amazon rain forest produce more than 20 percent of the world's **oxygen**.

On the floor

Barely any light reaches the rain forest floor where the canopy is thickest. Few plants grow here, and in some places the ground is bare except for a thin layer of dead leaves and twigs that have dropped from above.

Jungle giant

The African okapi is one of the tallest rain forest animals and it is related to the giraffe. It is nearly 6.5 feet (2 meters) tall, and can reach up to feed on the leaves of understory trees.

invertebrate
An animal that does not have a backbone, such as an insect.

This trapjaw ant has the fastest-shutting jaws of all animals.

Plenty of food

The forest floor provides food and shelter for a huge number of insects. Ants and other invertebrates live in the leaf litter or in the soil. These in turn are eaten by spiders, centipedes, and scorpions. Pigs and rats root among the litter. In turn, they are hunted by other animals higher up the **food chain**, such as snakes and big cats.

pupa of a trapjaw ant

- Less than 2 percent of the Sun's light reaches the forest floor.

- The okapi has a tongue that is so long it can lick its own eyelids.

- Leafcutter ants chew up leaves into a mush. The **fungus** that grows on the mush is the ants' food.

- The Goliath bird-eating tarantula can grow to 12 inches (30 centimeters) across—as big as a dinner plate.

- The maiden's veil fungus gives off a foul smell to attract flies, which spread the fungus's **spores**.

Fantastic fungus

Fungi play an important part in the forest. They feed on plant tissue and help break down the leaf litter. Mostly they are invisible, sending out tiny threads under the leaves, but occasionally they send threads up a stem or form structures that come in many shapes and colors.

maiden's veil fungus

leafcutter ant

The Goliath bird-eating tarantula is the largest spider in the world.

The understory

The rain forest understory is a mainly open space stretching from the floor up to about 66 feet (20 meters)—that's three times the height of a street lamppost. A few shrubs and small trees manage to grow here.

The tree kangaroo climbs by holding a branch with its front legs then hopping with powerful back legs.

The Burmese python has backward-sloping teeth that grip on to prey while the python's body crushes the prey to death.

On the up

The understory is home to animals that can fly in the open spaces or climb a short way into the trees. This includes a vast variety of birds, frogs, butterflies, and other insects. The largest **predators**, such as leopards and snakes, blend in with the dappled shade of the plants as they hunt birds and small mammals.

TOP FIVE BITESIZE FACTS

- The Burmese python's strongest sense is smell. It uses its tongue to "sniff" the air for prey.

- The Burmese python is one of the world's biggest snakes and grows to more than 16 feet (5 meters) long—about two and half times the length of a bed.

- Inside its hairy skin, the rambutan fruit is soft, juicy, and tasty.

- Flying foxes are the largest kind of bat and can weigh more than 2 pounds (1 kilogram)—about the weight of a 40 ounce (1 liter) bottle of soda.

- There can be 500,000 weaver ants in a colony.

The clouded leopard is so-called because its markings look like clouds.

The flying fox is not a fox at all, but a fruit-eating bat.

Heliconia is a plant related to the banana.

The rambutan fruit is covered with fleshy spines.

Weaving leaves

In Southeast Asia, colonies of weaver ants make their nests with leaves. Starting at the tip, they fold over a leaf edge, clasp it with their jaws, and "sew" it to the other side. Their thread is a silky substance produced by the ant larvae (young that have just hatched). The ants squeeze the larvae gently so that they produce the silk that attaches one side of a leaf to another.

colony
A number of creatures of the same species that live and work together.

The canary-winged parakeet has four toes on each foot (two facing forward and two facing backward), which help the bird cling to trees.

Crowded canopy

As well as the trees and their fruits, there are plants such as orchids, ferns, and **bromeliads**, which grow in cracks in the trunks and branches. Many animals like to live in the safety of the canopy where they find plenty of food.

Bromeliad leaves form a "tank" that collects rainwater.

The red howler monkey defends its territory by shouting and roaring.

A world in the air

The canopy is the roof of the rain forest. It can be 150 feet (45 meters) above the floor and forms an almost unbroken mass of leaves. The top part receives the full strength of the sunlight but shades the areas below. Inside the canopy is a dense network of branches, vines, and hanging plants.

The Amazon leaf frog keeps its eggs safe by wrapping them in leaves hanging over a river.

plumage
The feathers that cover a bird's entire body.

The three-toed sloth has fur that grows toward its spine, which allows rain to run off when the sloth hangs upside down.

The potoo has blotchy plumage and an unmoving stance that make it look like a tree branch.

TOP FIVE BITESIZE FACTS

- Many plant leaves are pointed so that rainwater can run off easily and **algae** do not grow.

- Scientists estimate that 60 to 90 percent of rain forest plants and animals are found in the trees.

- Animals living in the canopy have to fly, jump, or glide across the gaps between trees to move around the treetops.

- Scientists studying the canopy build walkways from tree to tree to move around.

- **Lianas** are plants that climb up other plants and trees, using them for support.

The spider monkey hooks its tail over a branch.

When threatened, large mouth opens wide and head points toward the threat.

Tail grips branch while snake grabs prey.

Slim climber

The green vine snake comes down from the canopy to hunt mice or small birds, before climbing back up to rest.

Treetop travel

The rain forest canopy is not just a home, but also a highway for many animals. Monkeys, snakes, anteaters, and even porcupines climb the trunks and travel along the branches. They have adapted so they can grab and cling to the trees and vines.

The fifth limb

Most climbing animals in the canopy have four limbs—two arms and two legs. But some, such as the South American spider monkey, have five. The fifth "limb" is their long tail, which has a movable tip. The spider monkey can bend the tip over and use it as a hook for swinging on branches.

TOP FIVE BITESIZE FACTS

- The spider monkey's tail is so strong that it can hold the monkey's entire weight.

- Spider monkeys live in groups, called troops, with up to 40 members.

- Green vine snakes can be 6.5 feet (2 meters) long, but less than 2 inches (1.5 centimeters) thick.

- When attacking, the vine snake bites into the prey's head and lifts the victim off the ground so that it is helpless.

- The vine snake injects **venom** to paralyze its prey before swallowing it whole.

With its hands safe around the branch, the monkey then lets go with its tail and swings forward.

Long arms reach out to grab another branch.

adapted
Changed over time to suit a new environment.

Feet that fly

All frogs have webs of skin between their toes, to help them swim. But some rain forest species, such as Wallace's flying frog, use these membranes to glide distances of longer than 30 feet (10 meters). This flying frog lives high in the jungles of Borneo and Thailand in Southeast Asia.

Fliers and gliders

Many jungle animals appear only at night. Flying creatures, such as bats, look for food. Some animals have adapted to the dark. They cannot actually fly, but use flaps of skin to glide.

Winged cradle

This colugo has a membrane that stretches from its shoulders to the tip of its tail. Spreading this out, the colugo can glide for more than 330 feet (100 meters.) When she is not flying, the female colugo uses the membrane as a cradle for her young.

Tail steering

The female sugar glider of Australia glides through the air using membranes between her arms and legs and steering with her tail. She has a pouch on her stomach in which her babies shelter.

TOP FIVE BITESIZE FACTS

🍃 Wallace's flying frogs have extra-long toes, so their membranes are much bigger than ordinary frogs. They also have flaps of skin on their sides.

🍃 The long toes of Wallace's flying frogs allow them to land softly and grip tree trunks.

🍃 Colugos grow to about 16 inches (40 centimeters) long and weigh up to 4.5 pounds (2 kilograms).

🍃 Sugar gliders can glide for up to 150 feet (45 meters) and can even catch moths and insects in mid-flight.

🍃 The fingers and toes of sugar gliders are like hooks so they can grab hold of tree trunks.

membrane
A thin layer of skin or tissue between two parts of the body.

When the flying frog jumps, it stretches out its toes, so the four feet act as wings.

The frog can change direction by extending or pulling back one of its limbs.

Hunters and prey

There are few large hunters in the rain forest and they are hard to spot. Hunters have to stay hidden, or their prey will see them. Leopards and other cats climb trees in search of food, or lie in the undergrowth. Other fearsome killers live on the forest floor.

Poison pump

The bushmaster snake of South America grows to more than 10 feet (3 meters) long. It has heat sensors on its head that detect warmth from other animals. Once it has caught the prey in its jaws, the snake injects deadly venom through its fangs.

Spotted coat mimics the dappled shade of the undergrowth.

Massive paws and sharp claws used to catch prey.

Death from above

The king vulture lives high in the canopy. It finds food by using its keen sense of smell, swooping on mammals or fish. Like other vultures, king vultures **scavenge** on dead creatures with their powerful beak.

prey
Animals that are killed and eaten by other animals.

Large ears pick up
the slightest sound.

Four large canine
teeth help grip
prey tightly.

Top cats

Cats live in the understory of
the rain forest. These are some
of the biggest and strongest of
all jungle animals. They are
called "top predators" because
they have no natural enemies.
The clouded leopard hunts
monkeys and squirrels.

TOP FIVE BITESIZE FACTS

🐾 The jaguar has the most powerful jaw muscles
of all cats.

🐾 A jaguar will ambush deer and other game
animals by leaping from the ground onto
their back.

🐾 Once leopards have killed their prey, they will
sometimes pull it up into a tree to keep it away
from scavengers.

🐾 Vultures have a bald head and neck. Any feathers
here would get clogged with blood as the birds
eat from the bodies of dead animals!

🐾 King vultures build their nests on the ground.

Water life

Rain forest rivers provide a home for lots of living things. Plants such as giant water lilies live here, as well as huge numbers of flies and other insects. There are also fearsome river hunters, including piranhas and caimans.

TOP FIVE BITESIZE FACTS

- Caimans have a see-through third eyelid that helps them to see while swimming underwater.

- Caimans can grow to 13 feet (4 meters) long—as long as a car.

- Piranhas have two rows of sharp teeth that they use to nip off chunks of flesh from their prey.

- The giant anaconda of the Amazon kills by wrapping its body around its prey and strangling it.

- Manatees can weigh as much as half a ton—about the weight of an adult male polar bear.

A caiman lies half-hidden in the water, waiting to ambush its prey.

piranha

ambush
To attack something by surprise from a hiding place.

Capybaras are the largest rodents and have webbed feet. They live in groups of 20 or more.

River visitors

Many animals are attracted to rivers, because they are rich in food as well as water. Land animals come to drink and swimmers visit to eat water plants or catch fish. Mammals such as capybaras or peccaries (a type of pig) make an easy meal for a caiman or snake.

River grazers

Manatees are large water mammals that eat mostly plants in shallow water. Manatees spend much of the day sleeping underwater, coming up to the surface to breathe every 20 minutes.

Rows of special organs on each side of the eel's body release electric charges into the water.

Amazon electric eels can produce electric shocks to stun prey or use as a defense.

Rain forest people

Humans have lived in rain forests for thousands of years. They have learned to make the best of the rich resources that can be found there. Many of these people hunt and gather all they need from the forest around them. Some have never had contact with the outside world.

staple food
The major part of a person's diet—usually a starchy food, such as cassava or potatoes.

Hunting for food

The rain forests are difficult places to find food but rain forest people have developed ways to survive. Some hunt animals for food. They use bows and arrows to shoot birds and monkeys, or nets and spears for larger animals such as deer.

A Ugandan pygmy hunts monkeys—a vital food source.

A village in one house

The Dayak people of Sarawak, Indonesia, have their homes in wooden longhouses. These are so big that a whole village of a dozen or more families can live together in one building.

Energy giving

Cassava (also called manioc) is a staple food of the rain forest people of South America and Africa. Its starchy roots grow well in poor soils and are a rich source of energy. Cassava is grated and crushed before cooking to get rid of its poisonous juices.

Ceremonial dress

Many people in the rain forest, such as this man from Papua New Guinea, decorate their body for special ceremonies. Decorations include body paint and large ornaments. These may indicate a person's importance, or act as charms to protect them from sickness or bring good harvests.

TOP FIVE BITESIZE FACTS

- Hunters in the Amazon use **blowpipes** and coat the tips of the darts with poison from the arrow frog.

- It is estimated that 50 million people live in the world's rain forests.

- There are up to 500 different tribes living in the Amazon rain forest.

- About 50 of these tribes have never had contact with the outside world.

- Some tribes live as **nomads**, moving from one place to another to find food and shelter.

23

Rain forest resources

Rain forests are full of many things that are vital to the planet. Some plants, such as rubber and cocoa, are now valuable crops. Many important medicines are produced from jungle plants. Spices, resins, and dyes also come from the rain forest.

Climate change

A quarter of the world's carbon is "locked" in rain forest plants. Humans burn vast areas of rain forest each year releasing carbon into the air. This adds to climate change, increasing natural disasters such as landslides and floods.

Flooding and landslides in the Philippines.

cocoa seeds

Researching the trees

Despite the hard work of scientists, there is still a lot we don't know about rain forests. For instance, how long is the full life cycle of a tree? There are no seasons in the tropics so trees do not show annual **growth rings**.

carbon
A substance that forms the gas carbon dioxide when trees rot down or are burned.

The biggest sugar cane producing countries are Brazil and India.

Food crops

Many foods that you see or eat each day come from rain forests. Sugar cane originally came from the forests of New Guinea. Today, it is one of the world's most important crops. Other rain forest foods include coffee, cocoa, bananas, ginger, and peanuts.

Coffee beans come from a tropical plant, and are now a major crop in South America and Southeast Asia.

Many plant species in tropical Kauai drifted to the island by sea and wind, or were carried by animals, including people.

TOP FIVE BITESIZE FACTS

- More than 65,600 square miles (170,000 square kilometers) of rain forest are destroyed each year —that's the same size as Florida.

- Scientists have found more than 2000 tropical forest plants that have anti-cancer properties.

- In the past 50 years, almost one-half of the world's rain forests have been cut down.

- Chocolate really does grow on trees! Inside cocoa tree pods are the seeds from which cocoa powder and chocolate are made.

- About 4 square miles (10 square kilometers) of rain forest may contain 1500 species of flowering plant and 750 tree species.

The unknown

Every year, several completely new species of plants and animals are discovered, but many are still unknown to us. As the rain forests are gradually destroyed, these creatures may be lost for ever. Scientists examine and record the species they find. However, the area covered by the world's rain forests is so huge that much of it is unexplored.

Disappearing wilderness

Tropical rain forests began to disappear many thousands of years ago. Early humans learned to clear land with fire and tools. Over the centuries, the rate of the destruction has grown faster. Today, people use machinery to flatten the trees.

deforestation
The cutting down and destroying of trees and other plants in a forest.

Setting fire to the trees is a quick way of clearing a rain forest.

Map of destruction

As this world map shows, some regions of rain forest (marked with flame symbols) have been more badly hit by deforestation than others. Among the worst affected are Brazil and parts of Indonesia, where vast areas are still being destroyed today.

Smoking ruins

There are many reasons why forests are cut down. Farmers want more land to raise cattle or grow crops. Loggers want the timber from the trees to make paper and other goods. As populations grow, towns expand into areas that were once wild. But once the cover of the trees has gone, the soil quickly loses its **nutrients**. Heavy rains wash out all the goodness and cause erosion.

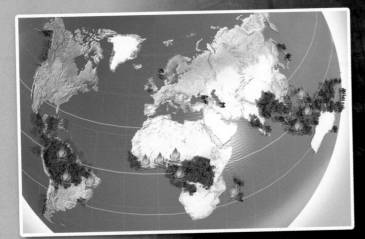

Super highway

Work on the Trans-Amazonian Highway in South America began in the 1970s. This giant road cuts straight through the rain forest. The Highway has opened up the area to even more logging and mining.

Cattle ranchers "slash and burn" large areas of forest and grow grass for herds of cattle to feed on.

Tigers in danger

As rain forests shrink and human settlements expand, many animals are losing their homes and hunting grounds. There are probably fewer than 2500 Bengal tigers alive today. They are being killed by **poachers** or by frightened villagers. This tigress was attacked when it strayed near a village in northeast India. It was rescued by forest workers, taken back into the rain forest, and then released.

A tigress leaps back into the wild.

The last rain forests

Centuries ago, there were approximately 9.6 million square miles (25 million square kilometers) of rain forest across the globe. Today, almost half of that vast area has gone—most of it in the past 50 years, due to human activity.

Hunting, war, and habitat loss from farming, logging, and charcoal production have reduced the number of red colobus monkeys.

Banana plantations, cattle ranching, and logging have destroyed much of the great green macaw's habitat.

Populations of the golden lion tamarin, increased by conservation projects, live in small pockets of recovering forest.

Slow growth

In some countries, seedlings of rare rain forest trees are planted to reforest areas, but many trees grow very slowly. Mahogany trees can take several hundred years to mature.

TOP FIVE 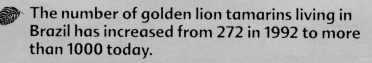 FACTS

- There are fewer than 2500 adult great green macaws left in Central America.

- The number of golden lion tamarins living in Brazil has increased from 272 in 1992 to more than 1000 today.

- There are only about 50 Javan rhinoceroses left in the wild.

- At the present rate of deforestation, the jungles of the world will have disappeared by 2060.

- There are fewer than 50,000 orangutans left in Southeast Asia,

extinct
No longer existing in a living form, having died out.

The Javan rhinoceros has lost habitat to farming and through poaching for its horn, which is valued in Asian medicine.

Chimpanzees suffer from poaching, disease, and loss of habitat to farms, logging, oil, and gas mining.

Loss of habitat to human interests (farms, roads, mines, settlements, logging, poaching) plus natural forest fires have had a bad impact on the numbers of orangutans.

Golden mantellas' habitat is threatened by logging, farming, settlements, and fire.

Tourism has affected the habitat of this tree frog and global warming makes its future uncertain.

Lost forever
The felling of a rain forest harms far more than the trees. Mammals, birds, insects, and reptiles lose their homes and food. These animals also disappear for good. Estimates show that 9000 species become extinct every year—most of them from rain forests. The destruction also threatens native peoples, who are driven out as the forests are cut down.

Glossary

algae
Single-celled plants that grow in water.

blowpipe
A long, narrow pipe through which a dart (small arrow) is blown.

bromeliad
A type of rain forest plant from the pineapple family that grows on trees.

canopy
The top layer of a rain forest.

emergent
A tree that sticks out above the canopy.

food chain
A series of living things that depend on each other for food. In the rain forest, a powerful predator such as a jaguar will be near the top of the food chain.

fungus
A type of living thing that does not have leaves, roots, or stems and reproduces using spores.

growth ring
The layer of wood produced by a tree in a temperate region, showing one year's growth.

habitat
The surroundings that a plant or animal lives in.

leaf litter
Dead leaves that fall to the floor. Nutrients from the leaves pass back into the soil.

liana
A type of woody plant that climbs up other plants, using them for support.

mammal
An animal that gives birth to live young, which feed on their mother's milk.

nomad
A person with no fixed home and who wanders in search of food.

nutrients
Substances that living things need to absorb in order to live and grow.

oxygen
A colorless gas in the atmosphere that is necessary for plant and animal life.

poachers
People who hunt animals illegally, for their meat, skins, tusks, or horns.

pollinate
To fertilize a plant by carrying a grain called pollen from a male plant to a

female plant. Pollen can be carried by wind, insects, or other animals.

predator

An animal that hunts and kills other animals.

reptile

A cold-blooded animal with scaly skin, for example a lizard. Some reptiles lay eggs, but others give birth to live young.

scavenge

To feed on the bodies of dead animals.

species

A type of living thing.

spores

A cell, a bit like a plant's seeds, from which a new fungus grows.

tropics

Regions that lie on either side of the Equator.

understory

The layer of a rain forest between the floor and the canopy.

venom

The poisonous fluid that some animals, such as snakes, inject into other creatures using fangs or stingers.

Index